HALLOWEEN: HALLOWED OR HEINOUS?

PATRICIA NORMAN RACHAL

NewCreationInspirations

HALLOWEEN

TABLE OF CONTENTS

Forward

There is a great deal of controversy that surrounds today's Halloween customs. To celebrate, or not to celebrate? *That* is the question in Christian circles today. Much of the controversy is because of confusion about the holiday. Some say it is a Christian holiday, others say it is Satan's holiday. Historical fact compared with Biblical exhortation sheds much light on the subject.

Halloween's seemingly innocent customs become dangerous when steeped in evil tradition. Surprisingly trick or treating and Jack-o-lanterns only assume the appearance of innocence. Some of the customs incorporate witchcraft and fortune telling. Many times it is only a pretense of these, but therein lies the deception. Celebrators, perhaps unknowingly, participate in festivals of death and darkness. Paganism and Christianity are blended for a compromise. When the facts are revealed, it becomes clear who can claim ownership of this holiday. Christians will be astonished how much we have compromised on the customs.

The Church no longer has to be divided or confused on the issue of typical Halloween celebrations. We have the tools and "glue" to mend the rift and remove the obscurity. There are alternatives without compromise. We can find our way back to agreement and unity by finding a final answer to the question, To celebrate or not to celebrate?

Whose Holiday is it Anyway?

Halloween is portrayed as an innocent holiday, but a typical celebration would include activities that are, in fact, culpable. A traditional party would include, among other things, fortune telling, relating stories of ghosts and witches, bobbing for apples, and dressing in costumes, frequently impersonating the characters those costumes depict. Halloween costumes might portray a witch or any number of horror subjects. One may have an upside down cross or other Halloween graffiti blatantly plastered across his forehead or, perhaps, 'blood' oozing from his mouth, eyes, or nose. On the other hand, a costume may represent something totally void of significant evil but when steeped in Halloween's tradition becomes shrouded in its evil.

Some people, both Christian and non Christian, say that Halloween is a Christian holiday, but it is definitely not Christ like considering the things associated with it. I remember a very popular rock singer deeply involved in the occult who said Halloween is her favorite night of the year. At many of her concerts, she dedicates the songs or the entire night to all the witches of the world. Considering the definite contrast between the occult and Christianity, it is very unlikely that Halloween would be her favorite holiday if it were a Christian holiday. (This is not an attack directed at the artist but merely an example for the sake of comparison.) On the other side of the coin, many Christian churches confess Jesus Christ as Lord while celebrating Halloween every October. Is it Satan's holiday or the Christians' holiday?

In the following paragraphs Halloween's historical facts and customs are discussed, as well as what God says applicable to Christians observing it. Under the scrutiny of God's Word, Halloween's tradition will no longer hide under the guise of innocence or Christianity but will be exposed for the infamous observance it really is. The true ownership of this controversial holiday will be elucidated.

What are some things that a typical Halloween party might include?

    1.

    2.

    3.

Who says Halloween is a Christian holiday?

    1.

    2.

What are your views on Halloween?

    1.

    2.

How can we find the answers to our questions?

    1.

    2.

Festivals of the Dead

Halloween developed from ancient New Year festivals and festivals of the dead. The Bible says in Leviticus, "The soul that turns after such as have familiar spirits, and after wizards, to go whoring after them—*spiritual idolatry*—I will even set my face against that soul and will cut him off from among his people."[1]

A familiar spirit is the spirit of a dead person called by a medium, to speak either through the medium or apart from the medium, the medium being the possessor or lord of that spirit.

Wizard is defined as one who professed to have the ability to converse with the spirits of the dead.[2]

This passage from Leviticus continues with clear, concise instruction. "Sanctify yourselves, therefore, and be ye holy, for I am the Lord your God...ye shall be holy unto me, for I, the Lord, am holy and have severed you from other people, that ye should be mine. A man or woman that hath a familiar spirit, or that is a wizard shall surely be put to death; they shall stone them with stones; their blood shall be upon them."[3] Halloween, therefore, with its development being partially from ancient festivals of the dead, cannot be pleasing to God, or hold a claim on the word "holy."

Paganism and Christianity

Grolier's Encyclopedia states:

> Now a children's holiday Halloween was originally a Celtic festival for the dead, celebrated on the last day of the Celtic year, 31 October. Elements of that festival were incorporated into the Christian holiday of All Hallows' Eve, the night preceeding All Saints' (Hallows') day. Until recent times in some parts of Europe, it was believed that on this night witches and warlocks (male witches) flew abroad, and huge bonfires were built to ward off these malevolent spirits. Children's pranks replaced witches' tricks in the nineteenth century, but most of the other Halloween customs are probably survivals from the Celtic Festival.[4]

In the AD 800s the church established All Saints' Day on 1 November so that people could continue a festival they had celebrated *before* becoming Christians. The evening before became known as Halloween. Many Celtic customs remained after people became Christians. They made old pagan customs part of the Christian holy day. Later they began to honor the dead on 2 November.

First Corinthians 10:21 very expressly confirms that paganism and Christianity cannot be mixed. It reads as follows: "Ye cannot drink the cup of the Lord and the cup of devils; ye cannot be partakers of the Lord's table and of the table of devils." Because of their origination, even the seemingly innocent customs should be avoided as Galatians 5:9 declares that even a *little* leaven leaveneth the whole lump. Leaven is a symbol of any evil influence, which if allowed to remain, can corrupt the Body of believers.[5] When spreading through the mass of that in which it is mixed, it symbolizes the *pervasive* character of evil. In the New Testament it is used metaphorically of corrupt doctrine and of error mixed with the truth.[6]

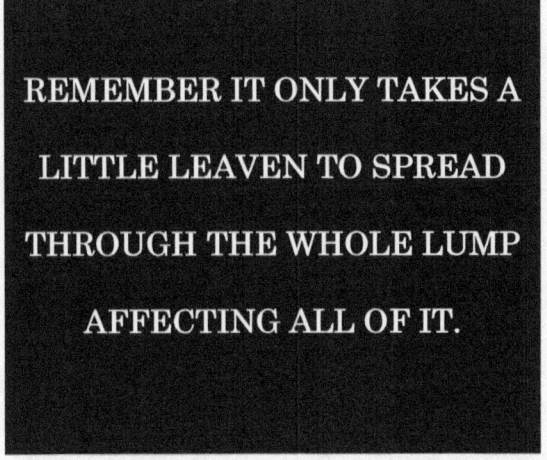

REMEMBER IT ONLY TAKES A LITTLE LEAVEN TO SPREAD THROUGH THE WHOLE LUMP AFFECTING ALL OF IT.

Treat, or Trick?

In spite of all the dangerous pranks pulled on our children over the years many still trick or treat. They are not really being treated, but tricked into an ungodly custom. One ancient custom had poor people going "a-souling" (begging). They received pastries called "soulcakes" in exchange for promising to say prayers for the dead.

An Irish custom has people begging for food in a parade that honored Muck Olla, a god. Some believe trick or treating originated from this custom. A celebration in honor of a god is the essence of service to that god.

Idolatry is so offensive to God, in the New Testament He commands us to flee from it, and in the Old Testament He admonishes us to have no other gods before Him.[7] Deuteronomy 13:6–11 tells us that if those we are most intimate with should try to entice us to honor another god we should not be persuaded even then.

Only verses 6–8a are shown here, but I encourage a reading of the entire passage. "If thy brother...or thy son, or thy daughter, or the wife of thy bosom, or thy friend which is as thine own soul entice thee secretly, saying, 'Let us go and serve other gods', which thou hast not known, thou nor thy fathers; namely of the gods of the people which are round about you, nigh unto thee, or far off from thee from the one end of the earth even unto the other end of the earth, thou shalt not consent unto him, nor hearken unto him..."

So here's the challenge: Do what everyone else is doing or educate ourselves on the customs and traditions and make an educated decision based on what we learn.

How do we do that? We can research historical facts. With the internet the world is in our hands with the touch of a button. We can find out anything we want to know. Almost everyone has a public library near them where reference books are readily available, as well as computers for those who don't own one.

God's Word is a roadmap for us. He tells us everything we need to know. It is up to us to read what He has put into our hands. From there we can ignore it or acknowledge it. The one unchanging factor in our lives is God and His Word. John 1:1 says the Word was with God in the beginning and was God. Verse 14 says the Word was made flesh and dwelt among us. Hebrews 13:8 says that Jesus Christ is the same yesterday, today and forever.

Therefore, when we read Deuteronomy 13 the commands haven't changed. We are to conform to them. It is easy to 'go with the flow' and forget how meaningful the Bible is to us. We feebly attempt to conform its instructions to our desired lifestyle. Considering the mess the world is in we should know it doesn't work that way.

Pray. Communication with God is vital. If we but ask, He will answer.

A Man Called Jack

Customary to Halloween are the bright, pumpkin-head Jack-O-Lanterns with their alluring, cozy lights flickering within. According to Irish legend, Jack-O-Lanterns were named for a man called Jack who could enter neither Heaven because he was a miser, nor Hell because he played tricks on the devil. Therefore, Jack had to walk the earth with his lantern until the Judgment Day. An interesting Scripture relative to this legend is found in Ecclesiastes 9:5–6 stating plainly that the dead have no participation in anything on the earth. With an origination so contrary to Jesus' own teachings that speak of fruit of the Spirit in Galatians 5 and love in 1 Corinthians 13, this custom definitely has some leaven in it too.

Witches, Ghosts, and Goblins

People once believed that ghosts roamed the earth on Halloween. It was also believed that all witches met on 31 October to worship the devil. Do witches really meet on this date? I have no documented proof of this, but, undoubtedly, ghosts and witches *are* symbolic of Halloween. God speaks strongly regarding witches. "Thou shalt not suffer a witch to live. There shall not be found among you anyone that makes his son or daughter to pass through the fire, or that uses divination, or an observer of times, or an enchanter, or a witch." He goes on to say that all that do these things are an abomination to the Lord. I am not implying that we as individuals should do anything to a person professing to practice witchcraft or divination—except tell them about Jesus. I only wish to make the point that God does say witchcraft is a sin, and we are to have nothing to do with it. First Samuel 15:23 says that rebellion is as the *sin* of witchcraft. We will also find witchcraft listed in the works of the flesh in Galatians. It is plain that they who do such things will not inherit the kingdom of God.[8]

Today many people do not believe in ghosts or witches; however, both remain symbolic of Halloween. If they were merely symbols, God would not have given such profound opposition in reference to them. Impersonating a ghost or witch, or subscribing to such things, is giving place to the devil who is very deceptive and capable of pulling innocent people into his ways by pretenses of incantations, rituals, and so forth. We should never play with witchcraft. People who play with fire get burned. Ephesians 4:27 says not to give place to the devil. Do not even let him get his foot in the door. Protect your children and yourself. Satan does not play fair and whoever plays his games will get hurt.

Goblins are adorable, cute little creatures when our children dress like them in their costumes. Another deception of the devil, for a goblin by definition (*Webster's*) is an evil or mischievous sprite. Sprite is derived from the same source as "spirit" and is defined as such a creature who is ethereal or disembodied and who lives in the air rather than on the earth. A goblin suggests a misshapen elf of repulsive appearance who is always conceived of as being malevolent toward human beings. A night creature, he is the companion of witches and the devil.[9] Is this what we want our children to embody?

Festivals of Death and Darkness
Incorporated Fortune Telling

The Celtic Festival of Samhain is probably the source of today's Halloween celebrations. The Celts New Year began on 1 November. A festival that began the previous evening honored Samhain, the Celtic lord of death. This festival marked the beginning of cold, darkness, and decay. God is light and has no darkness in Him. For us—as Christians—to associate ourselves with things of darkness makes us a liar.[10] The Festival of Samhain became associated with human death. Celts believed that Samhain allowed the dead souls to return to their earthly homes for this evening. As stated before (see A MAN CALLED JACK) this is contrary to scriptural teaching.

On the eve of the festival of Samhain, the Druids who were the priests and teachers of the Celts, ordered people to put out their hearth fires. The Druids then built a bonfire of oak branches, which they considered sacred. They sacrificed animals, crops, and possibly human beings in this huge bonfire. (See Lev. 18:21; Deut. 18:10; 2 Ki. 16: 2–4; Jer. 19:4–5) Then each family relit its hearth fire from the bonfire. Sometimes during this celebration they dressed in costumes made from animal skins and animal heads. If our present-day custom of dressing in costumes evolved from this practice, we would be wise not to allow our children to dress in them.

Then they told fortunes about the coming year by examining the remains of animals offered as sacrifices. There is a prime example of this in Ezekiel 21:21. "For the king of Babylon stood at the parting of the way, at the head of two ways to use divination; he made his arrows bright; he consulted with images; he looked in the liver." The footnote in the *Thomas Nelson Chain Reference Bible* and *New American Standard Bible* defines images as teraphim. *Smith's Bible Dictionary* defines teraphim as strange gods, articles of false worship, and objects of superstitious regard. Divination is an imitation of prophesy; the art of pretending to foretell future events from various items including the entrails of slaughtered animals and birds, especially the liver.[11] Sometimes the act of inspection of the intestines of animals is called augury and was common in Babylon.[12] Augury is also defined as the practice of divination from omens.[13]

God condemned divination by any means, but I cannot remember going to very many Halloween celebrations where someone was not playing the part of a diviner or fortuneteller. Fortune telling began in Europe hundreds of years ago. Today fortune-telling techniques used at Halloween include card reading and palmistry among other traditional methods. God talks about false prophets (ones who entice people away from Him) in the Bible and states in one verse that the false prophets should be put to death. He gives precise instruction concerning all sorts of fortune telling and then goes on to explain that He would send His prophet to speak by His Spirit. God also teaches that we should ask Him, rather than mediums or spiritists (fortunetellers), for instruction.[14] He honors His prophets and will not bless any false prophecy. Whether one calls it fortune telling, augury, clairvoyance, second sights, trance mediums, cards, divining rods, or palm reading it will bring God's judgment.

The Romans later conquered the Celts, and Roman festivals combined with the Celtic Samhain Festival. Feralia, held in late October, honored the dead. Another festival honored Pamona, a Roman goddess of fruit and trees. Bobbing for apples probably became associated with Halloween because of this.

Halloween Customs VS
Christian Practices

Many early American settlers came from Celtic regions bringing these customs with them, but because of the strict religious beliefs of other settlers, Halloween celebrations were not popular in the United States until the 1800s. These settlers were not willing to compromise their religious convictions or Christian beliefs. However, celebrating of Halloween became widespread and increasingly popular in the liberal 1900s. It continues to grow in millennial popularity.

Department store shelves are rife with Halloween and Christmas decorations displayed side by side. Is this some sort of sick satire? Just as ironic are the Halloween lights dressing up people's houses and lawns. I see more of them each year. I am all for Christmas lights for the Lord of Life but not Halloween lights for the Lord of Death. We, as Christians, should not leave room for such compromise. It is our responsibility to turn the trend back to what it was before the 1800s.

Consider the things associated with Halloween. Fortune telling, witches, ghosts, goblins, things indicative of violence, spook houses, darkness, death, and dirty tricks if we are not treated are all contrary to God's character and His Word. A comparison of the works of the flesh with the Spiritual fruit from Galatians 5:19–23 reveals clearly in which category Halloween belongs. Some of the deeds of the flesh are impurity, idolatry, sorcery, strife, and outbursts of anger, all of which could easily be associated with Halloween. Contrastingly, the fruit of the Spirit encompasses love, joy, peace, kindness, goodness, gentleness, and self-control, none of which can be associated with this holiday.

God says that we cannot be partakers of the Lord's table and the table of devils at the same time. The context of that passage is talking about immorality, idolatry, and sacrificing to idols and demons. The *NASB* actually says become sharers in demons. Another translation says partners with demons.[15] Wouldn't our participating in a typical Halloween celebration make us sharers in demons and partners with them? Remember, a little leaven leavens the whole lump.

Second Corinthians 6:14–16a asks some very specific questions, all of which have negative answers. "What fellowship has righteousness with unrighteousness? What communion has light with darkness? What concord has Christ with Belial? What agreement has the temple of God with idols?" None is the answer to each question. The concluding verses (16b–18) of that passage explain the reason each of those questions has a negative answer. "For ye are the temple of the living God...they shall be my people. Wherefore, come out from among them and be separate, says the Lord, and touch not the unclean thing, and I will receive you...be a Father unto you and ye shall be my sons and daughters..."

The Bible gives clear admonition to us as Christians how we should conduct ourselves. It shows the definite contrast between God's children and children of darkness.

My paraphrase of that admonition follows. "We are to be followers of God, walking in love as Christ loved us. Uncleanness and filthiness are not to be named among us. Idolaters have no inheritance in the kingdom of Christ and of God. Because of these things, God's wrath comes upon children of disobedience. We are not to be partakers with them. We are light in the Lord, no longer darkness as we once were. Therefore, we are to walk as children of light, for the fruit of the Spirit is in righteousness and truth. In this way, we will prove what is acceptable to the Lord. Rather than having fellowship with the unfruitful works of darkness, reprove them, for it is a shame even to speak of those things which are done of them in secret. Christ will give us His light. Walk carefully, redeeming the time, because the days are evil. Be not unwise but understanding what the will of the Lord is."[16]

■ **SOMETHING TO THINK ABOUT: WE DON'T HAVE TO BE PRIMITIVE TO MAINTAIN OUR BOND WITH THE AGELESS WORD OF GOD.**

Deception

Many who celebrate Halloween profess Christianity. Perhaps some are not aware that the celebrations are totally opposite Christian values. Satan prowls around looking for someone to pull into his wicked, sly schemes.

Is there any righteousness in this celebration? Any light? Definitely not! On the contrary, there is only unrighteousness and darkness. Why should we, the light of the world, associate in this manner with the ways of darkness? What agreement does Christ have with worthless, devilish things? Absolutely none.

We should wake up spiritually, realizing God lives and reigns in us, and come out from among them and be separate from wicked practices. There is no doubt in my mind that Halloween customs easily fit into the category of wicked practices.

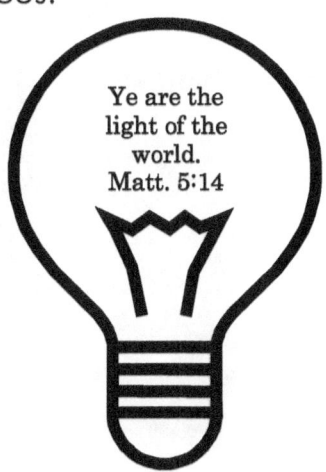

Ye are the light of the world.
Matt. 5:14

Christ our Example

Jesus left an example for us to follow. Would we find Him participating in a traditional Halloween celebration? Emphatically, no! Therefore, we should refrain from participating and, according to Scripture, be examples to others as He is to us.[17]

So, when you accepted the message, you followed our example and the example of the Lord. You suffered, but the Holy Spirit made you glad. You became an example for all the Lord's followers in Macedonia and Achaia. Everyone is talking about...how you turned away from idols to serve the true and living God. l Thess. 1:6, 7, 9 CEV

Submission is Ammunition

Submission to God and resistance to the devil causes him to flee from us. Participating in Halloween activities is not submitting to God, nor is it resisting the devil. The dark tradition of Halloween rather gives place to the devil and gives him a foothold in our lives.[18] We have the ammunition at our disposal, so why not avail ourselves to it?

> Likewise, ye younger, submit yourselves unto the elder. Yea, all of you be subject one to another, and be clothed with humility: for God resisteth the proud, and giveth grace to the humble.
>
> I Peter 5:5

Compensation Without Compromise

Halloween's popularity has grown to equal that of major holidays. Consequently, children are going to raise the question of why they cannot take part in the "fun". Today's stressed world certainly needs the therapy of fun, but we, as Christians, should use discernment and not intermingle fun with pagan customs epitomizing leaven (i.e., error and corruption). We should explain to our children, from God's perspective, why it is ungodly to take part in this holiday. They need to be reassured that we want God's best for them—that this is not a deprivation but a benefit to them spiritually. We should pray with our children regarding our own convictions and beliefs. They will most likely share the same beliefs when their parents bring them to an understanding of those beliefs and, as God works in them, the same convictions. This is ministry to our children. It establishes godly traditions we can pass down to our children, grandchildren, and future generations.

There are alternatives to typical Halloween celebrations. A number of churches now have a Harvest Fest or Fall Fest instead of a traditional celebration. However, in doing this, we still need to be careful not to revert to the same customary celebration under a different name. It would be good to incorporate evangelism, a "harvest of souls", into our Harvest Fest. Instead of trick or treating, go door to door sharing the gospel with people by handing out gospel tracts or some other means of communication. Another effective evangelistic outreach is drama—something youth do very well. This is one night we could almost be sure of salvaging someone's soul. Other suggestions for a fall festival might include a hayride with Christian entertainment or singing, a barbecue, or pizza party, not to mention the variety of creative ideas our youth have.

It would be awesome to have 31 October of every year set aside to glorify Christ instead of the devil. In fact, I find it rather encouraging that in the past few years I have noticed some churches having praise rallies or prayer vigils on this date. Another thing I have observed is that some groups choose to disregard Halloween altogether as a time of celebration. If Christians will stand together in this, perhaps, Halloween as we know it will begin to abate.

Satan's Power Overcome
By God's Power

There is no doubt those who are opposed to our opposition of Halloween. In light of this, consider Pharaoh's opposition to Aaron and Moses. God, by His power, turned Aaron's rod into a serpent. Pharaoh called his sorcerers and magicians. They, by Satan's power, turned the rods of Pharaoh's men into serpents. Nevertheless, the end proved victorious to God's people, for by His power Aaron's rod swallowed up the enemy's.[19] The enemy's opposing power holds no threat to the greater One who lives in us.[20]

Until God casts Satan into the place prepared for him, there will always be a battle between good and evil. God, of course, will be the ultimate winner. We are all prospective winners In Christ.

The Super Glue of Unity

Countless Scriptures, although not directly related to things of Halloween, can certainly be applied to holy living and complete dedication to God. One Scripture that sums up all of them is 1 Thessalonians 5:22 which says to abstain from all appearance of evil. Christians should always be ready to oppose, in a Godly manner, everything that has the appearance of evil. There has been compromise long enough. It is time for us to stand united together against evil bearing in mind the question Amos asked, "Can two walk together except they be agreed?" [21]

Hopefully we will come together in agreement with our Lord and each other that Halloween is, indeed, not hallowed since its tradition is cloaked in evil and ungodly beginnings. Certainly modern-day celebrations continue to don proudly that same cloak of evil.

Unity is to the Church as glue is to a model airplane. Once the glue comes into place all the pieces stick together, and it becomes a replica of the authentic airplane after which it was modeled. If the Church will stick together in unity and holiness and agree to abstain from taking part in heinous Halloween celebrations, we can become the model—the exact replica of Jesus—for others who are caught up in the confusion of to celebrate, or not to celebrate? [22]

Notes

All Scripture references are from the *King James Version Bible* unless otherwise noted.

Historical facts and customs are from *World Book Encyclopedia*, s.v. "Halloween", unless otherwise noted, used by permission.

1. Leviticus 20:6 (italics mine).
2. *Collins Gem Dictionary of the Bible,* s.v. "Familiar Spirit", "Wizard."
3. Leviticus 20:7, 26–27.
4. *Groliers Multimedia Encyclopedia*, s.v. "Halloween", Grolier, Inc., 2003, <http://gme.grolier.com>, 3 April 2003 (second parenthetical words mine; much more can be revealed by an exhaustive study of the subject and its related articles).
5. *Holman's Bible Dictionary*, s.v. "Leaven."
6. *Vine's Expository Dictionary of Biblical Words*, s.v. "Leaven" (italics mine).
7. 1 Cor. 10:14; Exod. 20:1–5; 23:13, 24, 32–33; Deut. 8:19; 16:22–17:7 (there are numerous verses on the subject which can be researched using a concordance).
8. Exod. 22:18; Deut. 18:10–12; Gal. 5:19–21 (witchcraft/sorcery and divination/fortune telling are sometimes used interchangeably in various versions of the Bible; *Complete Jewish Bible* renders Galatians 5:20 "involvement with the occult and drugs...")

9. *Webster's New World Dictionary*, s.v. "Goblin"; *Reader's Digest Use the Right Word: A Modern Guide to Synonyms*, s.v. "Sprite."

10. 1 John 1:5–6.

11. *Smith's Bible Dictionary*, s.v. "Teraphim", "Divination", used by permission (Smith gives an excellent and thorough exposition on both words in the definitions' entirety); Collins Gem Dictionary of the Bible, s.v. "Divination."

12. See note 2, *Collins*, s.v. "Magic" (a very thorough definition of magic expounds upon many of the things discussed in this book).

13. See note 9, *Webster's*, s.v. "Augury."

14. Deut. 13:1–5; 18:9–22; Is. 8:19–20; Lev. 19:31; 2 Ki. 23:24.

15. 1 Corinthians 10:20–21, *New American Standard Bible,* Holman Bible Publishers, 1977; *Holman Christian Standard Bible,* 2000, Holman Bible Publishers, used by permission.

16. Ephesians 5:1–17.

17. 1 Thessalonians 1:7–9; 1 Peter 2:21 (the subject content is different, but the principal applies in every area of our lives).

18. James 4:7; Ephesians 4:27.

19. Exodus 7:10–13.

20. 1 John 4:4.

21. Amos 3:3; Ps. 133:1; Eph. 4:1–6 (3).

22. See note 17.

These books are available by author at Amazon.com, CreateSpace eStore and other retailers:

Halloween: Hallowed or Heinous?
The Light in the Valley

If you prefer, you may contact the author at proofnedit@inbox.com to place your order. Books are the same price either way.

eBooks available at Smashwords.com and other retailers:

Halloween: Hallowed or Heinous?
The Light in the Valley
God's Glorious Symphony
GhiAna's Jewels
Rhythms of Love
Reflections of the Son

Today's Halloween customs are quite controversial many times causing confusion and conflict. To celebrate, or not to celebrate? That is the question in many Christian circles today. Much of the controversy is because of confusion about the holiday. Some say it is Christian, others say it is Satan's holiday. Historical fact compared with biblical exhortation sheds much light on the subject. The Church no longer has to be divided or confused on the issue of typical Halloween celebrations. We have the tools and "glue" to mend the rift and remove the obscurity. Find your answers in Halloween: Hallowed or Heinous?

Mrs. Rachal has been writing since her conversion to Christianity on October 30, 1980, and attended Word of Life School of Ministry in Shreveport, LA. She says her greatest inspiration comes from within as a result of the 'new creation experience' of 2 Corinthians 5:17-21. One of her strongest convictions is that God sets the standard in HIS Word and we are to conform to the standard He sets, not feebly attempt to conform His Word to our desired lifestyles.

Mrs. Rachal has been the recipient of various poetry awards and has published six eBooks and two books in print.

ISBN 9781460935057

90000 >

9 781460 935057